The Marital Choice

A Compelling Look At
The Factors That Impact Selectivity

Scott Publishing Corporation
222 N. Columbus Drive
Chicago, Illinois 60601
312.217.2732

damon.m.scott@themaritalchoice.com

Coming soon!
The Marital Choice™ will be available at www.themaritalchoice.com.
Examine your relationship-decisions online at www.selectivityexam.com.

The Marital Choice: A Compelling Look At The Factors That Impact Selectivity
Copyright © 1999 by Damon M. Scott
The Selectivity Exam and The Comparative Analysis Model patent pending

All rights reserved, including the right of reproduction in whole or in part in any form. No part of this publication may be reproduced, stored in a retrieval system, or transmitted, in any form or by any means, electronic, mechanical, photocopying, recording or otherwise, without the prior express written consent of the publisher and author.

Manufactured in the United States of America
Printed in Mansfield, Ohio by BookMasters, Inc.
Set in 10 point Adobe Garamond font

First Edition 2003

The Martial Choice™ and all of its formulas are trademarks of Damon M. Scott

10   9   8   7   6   5   4   3

Library of Congress Cataloging-in-Publication Data
Scott, Damon Maurice, date.
The Marital Choice: A Compelling Look At The Factors That Impact Selectivity
ISBN   0-9746103-0-5
1. Selectivity 2. Marriage 3. Choice 4. Standards 5. Privilege 6. Decision
7. Decision-making-process 8 Relationship-decisions 9. Marital Choice
10. Marital-selection-process

The Marital Choice™ is available at special discounts for bulk purchase by conferences, single ministries, book clubs, and other organizations. For more information call 312-217-2732 or contact the author directly at damon.m.scott@themaritalchoice.com.

Acknowledgments

I would like to thank the following for contributing to my experience in writing this book.

First and foremost I must thank God for doing in three months what had taken me more than four years. You are truly a rewarder of them that diligently seek you. Also, thanks for honoring my confessions of faith and for causing me to deal wisely with the affairs of life.

A tremendous thanks to the plethora of those I interviewed for your neighborly engagement and for the pleasure of your conversations.

A spirit-filled thanks to my sister, Minister Clairetha Scott, for more than twenty years of intercessory prayer and for directing me to study the Bible in a way that allowed me to see the patterns in God's selection-decisions. Wow!

My sincerest gratitude to Shannon Verner who, by being my sounding board for ideas, exam questions, and conclusions over the years, contributed selflessly to this Socratic project.

Thanks also to Bryant & Melinda Scott, Trinette Scott, Marcus Schlemmer, Darice Caudle, Paul & Susan Schlemmer and their wedding party, Tanya at Bronxpages, Joycelyn Ward, Victoria Lewis, Rosey Brady, Keith White, Kirk & Diane Bradley and their wedding party, Dr. Jeffery O. G. Ogbar, Erin St.Onge, Keith Maull, Natalie Nelson, and Rick Packard (*yes indeedy!*).

Damon M. Scott

A special and enduring thanks to John & Alberta Scott, Mr. Leon Kendrick, Dr. Howard Hill, Dr. Richard Taatgen, Dr. James Mumford, and Atty. Gary D. Gold, CPA.

The Marital Choice™ was written over the course of four years, in scores of interviews, and hundreds of conversations, on phones, through emails, in clubs, restaurants, bars, bookstores, coffee houses, law firms, on consulting engagements, at parties, cook-outs, weddings, receptions, get-togethers, on planes, trains, automobiles, in Pittsburgh, Los Angeles, Santa Monica, Chicago, New York, Brooklyn, Atlanta, and Dallas.

The intent was to answer one question. Are men more or less selective than women when choosing marital partners? The response was amazing.

I interviewed an older woman who said that in her day not only was it popular for a woman to get married to get out of the house but that it was more popular for a woman to be a doctor's wife than a doctor. I also interviewed a younger woman who was a doctor and owned her own home. I have learned a lot about the changing times.

While waiting for gift-wrapping in New York I interviewed a man who said that, "…women know more about what men need than men themselves". On the other hand, I interviewed a woman in Chicago who said that women don't know what they want and that most women get married to have someone take care of them. I have heard many polarizing responses.

I interviewed a woman from Detroit who explained in earnest why men were more selective than women when choosing sexual partners. I also interviewed a consultant in Los Angeles who said that women were more selective than men when choosing marital partners because, "they grow up thinking about marriage". I have been exposed to an extraordinary breadth of reasons and perspectives.

One woman told me, "I got married because I wanted to have a family. I was not in love with my husband at the time but I was ready to be married". So many people told me if they had a chance to do it all over they would not marry the same person or get married for the same reason, which was extraordinary to relay to someone they had only just met. I have been exposed to an extraordinary level of frankness, honesty, and ingenuousness.

I have seen the wheels of a lawyer turn as she split hairs to decide if she would rather for her mate to treat her like a woman or like an equal. I have seen the expressions of hundreds of people as they grapple with questions about their standards and the integrity with which they apply them. I have been exposed to many honest moments with the human spirit.

I took the hundreds of answers I received, prayed about their commonalities, and examined them carefully for discernible patterns. The Marital Choice™ is the result of my analysis. Eventually it became apparent to me that there was a process in place to which all of the responses were subject, and that each response reflected a unique experience in that process. The Marital Choice™ is a conceptual draft of that process.

Thanks so much to everyone that participated, many of whom I didn't even know your names. For instance, I met a professor in New York who was Catholic, whose wife was Agnostic, that felt that religion played no role in his marital choice, and I didn't even know his name. I found, as many researchers have found, that anonymity is often the price of candor, particularly when people are sharing feelings about their marriages. With people bearing bits and pieces of their souls it is not possible for any contribution to be insignificant. Thank you so much for trusting me and for contributing to The Marital Choice™ with your openness and honesty.

Orchids to you...
Damon M. Scott
Chicago, IL

Prologue

The difference between life's boldest accomplishments and its most staggering failures is often, simply, the diligent will to persevere.
                                        -Abraham Lincoln

The Marital Choice™ is about something far more important than marriage. And what could be more important than marriage than something that existed before it: **choice**. The Marital Choice™ provides you with a look at the patterns in your relationship-decisions through use of:

- a discussion about the factors that impact selectivity, and
- a selectivity exam to inspect your relationship decisions.

The intent is to help you analyze the patterns in your relationship-decisions *before you make a marital choice*. Just as your life is the sum of your **choices**, the quality of your experience in your relationships is a result of the quality of your **choices**. If you can identify and correct any counterproductive patterns in your relationship-decisions before you **choose** a marital partner, then you can drastically increase the quality of your relationships and literally save the rest of your life.

The marital-selection-process also includes external factors that impact your selectivity. By getting a good look at these factors and the patterns in your relationship-decisions you gain both a prospective and an introspective view of the marital-selection-process. The Marital Choice™ takes no interest in who you marry. Rather, it takes an interest in you having an impeccable decision-making-process where your relationships are concerned. If your decision-making-process is solid, then making the right marital choice will be easy.

Even if you are engaged, however, it is not too late. If your conscience can survive the Selectivity Exam™ and the comparative analysis section then chances are you have made the right **choice**. Here is your chance to get a good look at the patterns in your relationship-decisions, particularly if you are having doubts or if your family and friends do not seem genuinely enthused. John F. Kennedy said, "an error doesn't become a mistake until you refuse to correct it'. **Choices** are long lasting and life altering. **Choose** wisely. The Marital Choice™ will help you determine if:

- you have standards but are not exercising them,
- your standards are too high or too low,
- your standards are commensurate with your privilege.

The Marital Choice™ also makes introspection enjoyable. Whether you are at dinner with a group of friends, at a book club meeting, or on the phone with your best friend, The Marital Choice™ enkindles piercing, thoughtful discussions and brings heartfelt amusement to groups and individuals alike. Good luck with your **choices** and enjoy your read!

The Marital Choice™ starts with your opinion!

Please answer the Selectivity Exam™ pre-test questions on the next page before you start your read. Nothing matters more than your opinion because your experience will be determined by how your answers are reconciled to the book. Comparing your answers to the theories advanced in the book will be the beginning of a fascinating relationship with the topic of selectivity. Be sure to circle your answer to each question and explain your position in earnest. Good luck and enjoy your exam!

SELECTIVITY EXAM™ PRE-TEST

1. Would you say that women are more or less selective than men when choosing sexual partners?
   a. more
   b. less

   Why?

2. Would you say that men are more or less selective than women when choosing marital partners?
   a. more
   b. less

   Why?

3. How selective are you?
   a. highly
   b. above average
   c. average
   d. below average
   e. low

   Why?

The unexamined life is not worth living.

Socrates

TABLE OF CONTENTS

Chapter 1 *page 17*
SELECTIVITY DEFINED

There is a difference between deciding what you want and getting what you want. Having standards means that you have decided what you want. Being selective means that you have the ability to get what you want. Selectivity is defined as Standards + Privilege = Selectivity™ with privilege being the enabler that turns a standard into a selection-choice.

Chapter 2 *page 25*
THE PRIVILEGE OF UNFETTERED CHOICE

The privilege of unfettered choice is the advantage of final authority. Gender provides women with the privilege of unfettered choice when choosing sexual partners. As a result, a man can only have sex with a woman that allows while a woman has the privilege of determining whom she will allow to have sex with her.

Chapter 3 *page 29*
THE RELATIONSHIP-SELECTION-PROCESS

There are two roles in the relationship-selection-process from which two decisions are made. The selection-decision is made from the active role and the standard-decision is made from the passive role. The selection-decision selects while the standard-decision evaluates, accepts, or declines. Selectivity is exercised from the active role while standards are exercised from the passive role.

Chapter 4 *page 31*
THE MARITAL-SELECTION-PROCESS &
THE PRIVILEGE OF UNFETTERED CHOICE

The sociological norms that govern the marital-selection-process dictates that the man should propose to the woman. In doing so, the norm places men in the active role of the marital-selection-process while placing women in the passive role. Being in the active role contributes to giving men the privilege of unfettered choice when choosing marital partners.

Chapter 5 *page 35*
WHY MEN ARE MORE SELECTIVE THAN WOMEN
WHEN CHOOSING MARITAL PARTNERS

Men are more selective than women when choosing marital partners because the marital-selection-process is not designed for women to make selection-decisions and because the symbolic value women place on commitment gives men the privilege of unfettered choice when choosing marital partners.

TABLE OF CONTENTS

Chapter 6 *page 43*
THE SELECTIVITY EXAM™

How selective are you? The exam asks questions about your privilege and standards to assess your level of selectivity. The exam also asks specific questions about your relationship-decisions to give you an opportunity to inspect your decision making process. Here is your chance to take a careful look at your relationship-decisions. Are you happy with your choices?

Chapter 7 *page 57*
THE COMPARATIVE ANALYSIS MODEL

Comparative analysis is designed to illuminate patterns in your relationship-decisions. The objective is to get you to consider if you would be comfortable making a marital choice with your current pattern of relationship-decisions? Do you have standards? Do you exercise your standards? Are your standards too low or too high? Are you settling? Are there any counterproductive patterns in your relationship-decisions? Comparative analysis is designed to help you answer these questions. The comparative analysis concluding questions are introduced. Have I decided to… ? Is that decision acceptable? What decision would be acceptable? How can I position myself to make that decision?

Chapter 8 *page 65*
PRIVILEGE & THE POWER OF THE PASSIVE ROLE

Privilege has the same impact in the passive role as it does in the active role: it is an enabler that turns a standard into a standard-choice. The primary benefit of being in the passive role is having the power to reject anyone that does not measure up to standards and being able to accept the person that does.

Chapter 9 *page 73*
THE IMPACT OF LOVE ON SELECTIVITY

One of the most fascinating aspects of being in love is that it frees you from want. Love factors standards out of the selection process eliminating the need for selectivity.

Chapter 10 *page 75*
THE ORIGIN OF THE MARITAL-SELECTION-PROCESS

With the fall of man from the Garden of Eden the marital-selection-process was created. The fall of man provided two requirements that are essential for the marital-selection-process to thrive: uncertainty as to whether people would connect and uncertainty about the quality of people available to connect.

TABLE OF CONTENTS

Chapter 11 *page 83*
EPILOGUE

Seven success factors are identified. The effect of seeing these factors should be similar to the effect of seeing the results of a budget for the first time. You learn valuable information about how you are allocating your resources. Are you happy with what you have learned?

Glossary *page 87*

Chapter 1:
Selectivity Defined

Standards + Privilege = Selectivity™

-Damon M. Scott

You know... it's touching. At many things in life we laugh because they're funny but also we laugh because they're true. Many people believe, incorrectly I might add, that they are selective because they have high standards, when nothing could be further from the truth. Having standards does not make you selective because there is a difference between deciding what you want and getting what you want. Having standards means that you have decided what you want. Being selective means that you have the ability to get what you want. The ability to get what you want requires an essential element of selectivity called privilege.

There are two elements required to be selective: ***standards*** and ***privilege***. The purpose of a standard is to determine adequacy, sufficiency, or acceptability. As such, standards comprise part of the voluntary portion of selectivity because only you can determine what is adequate or sufficient for you. Privilege can be both a voluntary and involuntary component of selectivity. Privilege can come from voluntary factors such as wealth, success, or prestige, or from involuntary factors such as attractiveness or personality. Loosely interpreted, privilege is what you have going for yourself. Technically, privilege enables you to get what you want, and it has both internal and external sources. For example, internal sources of privilege include being strikingly attractive, having the gift of gab, or a magnetic personality. External sources of privilege include having wealth, power, or factors such as social norms and being in specific roles in the relationship-selection-process. Each of these factors increases your ability to get what you want.

The Marital Choice

Selectivity works like this. Privilege is needed to exercise choice at a level commensurate with your standards. All things considered equal, the higher your standards the more privilege needed to exercise your selection-choice. For our purposes, selectivity is defined as:

Standards + Privilege = Selectivity™

In order to know how selective you are you must take into consideration both your standards and privilege. The most aggravating fact to accept about selectivity is that it has an involuntary component, which means that we do not have total control over how selective we can be. The most humbling fact to accept about selectivity is that many, if not most, of us do not have the privilege to be as selective as we would like to be. Those of us who have such privilege realize its power and are envied greatly. Many people feel that having high standards means that they are selective because they assume that selectivity contains only the voluntary component, standards, and that they have total control over that component. Nothing could be further from the truth.

Both standards and privilege are components of selectivity but privilege is much more important to being selective. Privilege is the primary determinant of selectivity because it provides **choice**, which is the essence of selectivity. Think of standards as your shopping-list and privilege as your money. When you have money you have options regardless of whether you have standards or not. The same is true for privilege. If you have the privilege of being strikingly attractive you have options whether you have standards or not. By providing options privilege provides choice. Let's consider a practical example of how selectivity works and equate that example to the marital-selection-process.

Consider O.J. Simpson. Once the slow-speed chase was over and Mr. Simpson was placed in custody, he knew he had an important selection decision to make. He had to select an attorney. Because of the seriousness of the charges and the consequences associated with a guilty verdict, he knew he had to select the best criminal defense attorney in Los Angeles. His standards were high, exceedingly high, for his selection-decision. Let's consider his privilege. O.J. Simpson was a famous, wealthy, Heisman trophy winning, Hall of Fame running back. He had substantial privileges at his disposal to assist him in making a selection-choice. Among his privileges were wealth and fame. As a result, he was able to hire a legal dream-team that included two of this nation's best criminal defense attorneys. Because his privilege exceeded his standards he was able to make a selection-choice that met or exceeded his highest standards.

Let's assume he was not famous or wealthy, and had no privilege to assist him when making his selection-choice. Would he have been able to hire his legal dream-team? Absolutely not! What difference would his high standards make without the privilege to exercise his choice? Without privilege he would have had to exercise a choice of lesser standards, such as being represented by fewer attorneys of less stature. Or worse, he would have had high standards while only being able to afford someone with little or no experience. He was able to make a selection-choice with high standards because he had high privilege.

The Marital Choice

Selective decisions are those where your privilege is greater than or equal to your standards, no matter how high your standards. For our purposes, decisions where privilege is greater than or equal to standards is expressed as:

$$P \geq S = \text{Selective}^{TM}$$
Where P = privilege, S = standards

Equating this expression to a marital choice, if your privilege meets or exceeds your standards then you have as much or more to offer your mate than you want in return. As a result, you have the ability to select a person that meets or exceeds your highest standards but not your privilege. For example, a star athlete, super-model, or movie star has the ability to select a person that meets or exceeds their highest standards because they are typically among the most privileged in terms of wealth, aesthetics, and fame.

Decisions that are not selective are those where your standards exceed your privilege. For our purposes, a decision where standards exceed privilege is expressed as:

$$S > P = \text{Not Selective}^{TM}$$
Where P = privilege, S = standards

Equating this expression to a marital choice, if your standards exceed your privilege, then you want more from your mate than you have to offer. As a result, you do not have the ability to select a person that meets your standards, but you do have the ability to select a person that meets your privilege. For instance, if you want your partner to be more accomplished, reliable, or have more integrity than you, then by definition you are less accomplished, reliable, or have less integrity, which comparatively decreases your privilege and therefore your ability to make a choice that meets or exceeds your highest standards. Your lack of privilege is limiting the amount of selectivity you can exercise.

Settling is a class of decision where neither privilege nor standards are fully utilized when exercising choice. The fundamental assumption in both of the previous decision making models is that one, if not both, of the key factors are fully utilized when making a selection choice. The model assumes that standards will always be at maximum levels to indicate that people will always prefer more to less. The model also assumes that privilege will always be at high to maximum levels to commensurate standards used in the selection-decision. When a person has settled they have made a decision that does not meet their privilege or their standards. They have neither what they want nor anything equivalent to what they have to offer.

Marrying down is a class of decision that is different than settling, though the two are perceived to be the same. A person marries down when their standards are commensurate with their partner's, though their privilege, by definition, is far superior. The equity in standards is what makes marrying down different than settling. People that settle know their mate does not meet their standards, which is not the case when someone marries down. However, when someone says, "they could have done so much better" about a person that married down, what they are really saying is that that person had the privilege to make a marital choice with higher standards but chose otherwise. The person that married up, on the other hand, is considered fortunate, lucky, or insincere because the perception is that their level of privilege could not have supported their marital choice, which also is not entirely accurate.

The Marital Choice

The funny thing about selectivity is that many people claim to be selective without knowing what being selective entails. And it is usually the people who want more than they have to offer that claim to be the most selective. Notwithstanding that, everyone has an idea of what they want even if they don't know why they want it. Understanding what they have to offer may be difficult because an accurate self-image is required. Privilege comes in many ways, however. Beauty, style, personality, innocence, wealth, brilliance, faith, confidence, talent, sex appeal, power, integrity: each of these attributes come with varying degrees of privilege. Each privilege is different for each gender. Attractiveness is a prime privilege for women because men are stimulated, primarily, by what they see. Wealth and power, on the other hand, rank as a prime privilege for men because many women are magnetically drawn to affluence and the perception of security.

**Chapter 2:
The Privilege of Unfettered Choice**

The natural superiority of woman is a biological fact, and a socially acknowledged reality.
-Ashley Montague

One attribute, more than any other, provides extraordinary privilege when exercising choice: gender. Let's examine the privilege gender provides for women. Anecdotal evidence suggests that men will always pursue women for sex more than the contrary. The imbalance in demand provides the female gender with an extraordinary advantage called the **Privilege of Unfettered Choice** when choosing sexual partners.

The privilege of unfettered choice is an advantage that results from the inefficiency in the process by which men and women interact. The privilege provides one gender with an advantage over the other. In short, the privilege of unfettered choice means that you have the final say over whether something happens or not. In this case, the inefficiencies inherent in the process by which men and women pursue sex favor women. As a result, a man can only have sex with a woman that allows while a woman has the privilege of determining whom she will allow to have sex with her. This does not mean that a woman can sleep with any man she wants. It does mean, however, that of the men interested in sleeping with her that she has the privilege of unfettered choice when choosing among them, or the final say in whether they sleep with her or not. This is the benefit of having the privilege of unfettered choice when choosing sexual partners. Women have it and men do not. The implication is that this is why men are much more likely than women to have sex with someone they do not love. Women have more privilege to exercise when choosing sexual partners. As a result, women have the advantage of being more selective than men when choosing sexual partners.

The Marital Choice

Sexual Choice™
$P_f > P_m$

P_f equals female privilege
P_m equals male privilege

ANOMALY

A highly privileged male is an anomaly. The privilege in his sexual choices will usually exceed the privilege in the sexual choices of most women. The most visible examples include professional athletes and/or recording artists that are extremely attractive and wealthy.

Chapter 3:
The Relationship-Selection-Process

There are two roles in every relationship-selection-process, from which two decisions are made. The first is the **_active role_** from which the **_Selection-Decision_** is made. The second is the **_passive role_** from which the **_Standard-Decision_** is made. The person making the selection-decision chooses or _selects_, while the person making the standard-decision _evaluates, accepts, or declines_. Selectivity is exercised with the selection-decision while standards are exercised with the standard-decision. Essentially, it is not possible to exercise selectivity from the passive role because the passive role does not select. The passive role evaluates, accepts, or declines, which is an exercise in standards. Selectivity is exercised from the active role in the selection-process. Now, let's examine the privilege gender provides for men.

**Chapter 4:
The Marital-Selection-Process &
The Privilege of Unfettered Choice**

He that finds a wife finds a good thing and obtains the favor of the Lord.
-Proverbs 18:22

Damon M. Scott

Have your parents ever told you, "choose your friends and don't let your friends choose you?" If so, your parents were telling you to take an active role in the selection of your friends and not a passive role. The inference is that you have more control over the outcome from the active role. The sociological norms that govern the marital-selection-process dictates that the man should propose to the woman. In doing so, the norm places men in the active role of the marital-selection-process while placing women in the passive role. Being in the active role contributes to giving men the privilege of unfettered choice when choosing marital partners in two ways.

First, the marital-selection-process is not designed for women to make selection-decisions; it is designed for women to be selected and for women to exercise their standards in response to being selected. It is not possible for a woman, or anyone, to be selective from the passive role. From the passive role a woman can exert influence but she can only marry a man that proposes while a man in the active role can propose to any woman *he chooses*. This does not mean that a man can marry any woman he wants. It does mean, however, that of the women interested in receiving a proposal from him that he has the privilege of unfettered choice, or the final say, over whether a proposal is extended or not. This is the benefit of having the privilege of unfettered choice when choosing marital partners. Men have it and women do not. The implication is that this is why women are much more likely than men to marry someone they do not love.

Second, the norm creates inefficiency in the marital-selection-process by preventing many women from proposing. The process is designed for women to be honored by being selected. The honor in being selected comes from the act of a man placing his honor at the mercy of a woman's standards by proposing, presumably on bended-knee. In order for a woman to be selective she would have to propose, which would mean placing her honor at the mercy of a man's standards. The very thought of such an act is repulsing to many women who feel that receiving a proposal is their rite-of-passage. To honor or to be honored? That is the question that women must resolve when deciding whether or not to propose, if this is a consideration at all.

Deciding not to propose increases the privilege men have to exercise in the marital-selection-process by increasing the relative importance of the proposal. Both factors,

- being in the active role of the marital-selection-process, and
- the inefficiency that prevent women from proposing,

increase the privilege men have to exercise in the marital-selection-process and contribute to giving men the privilege of unfettered choice when choosing marital partners. As a result, men have the advantage of being more selective than women when choosing marital partners.

Many women have remarked, "men cannot be more selective than women when choosing marital partners because they tend to marry the first woman that comes along when they are ready". This is true, and for the most part this is exactly how men behave. In emphasizing timing over standards, however, the critique overlooks the privilege of being able to make such a decision with such convenience. That a man could marry "the first woman that came along when he was ready" is an exercise in privilege that women do not have. This is the clearest example of the power of being in the active role of the marital-selection-process and having the privilege of unfettered choice when choosing marital partners.

There is one other major factor that contributes to giving men the privilege of unfettered choice when choosing marital partners. The factor is discussed in the next chapter.

Chapter 5:
Why Men Are More Selective Than Women When Choosing Marital Partners

Men are more selective than women when choosing marital partners because the marital-selection-process is not designed for women to make selection-decisions. It is designed for women to be honored by being selected and for women to make standard-decisions in response to being selected. And even when a woman does seize the active role in the process and propose, the active role does not provide as much privilege for her as it does for a man because men place very little, if any, symbolic value on commitment. Let's drill down to the detail of this explanation.

To compare the selectivity of a man to the selectivity of a woman you must place both in the active role of the marital-selection-process and gauge the privilege provided to each. To conclude that one gender is more selective than the other you must establish that the privilege provided to one as a result of being in the active role exceeds the privilege provided to the other. To do that you must identify the source of the privilege provided by the active role. That source is *the value of the proposal to the person in the passive role.*

If the person in the passive role wants to get married or longs for a proposal the probability of the proposal being accepted increases. The increased probability equates to an increase in privilege for the person in the active role. So, for example, any woman that has ever said, "I am really ready to get married" or "the next man I sleep with will be my husband" is increasing the privilege the person in the active role has to exercise. The privilege afforded the person in the active role is proportionate to the value of the proposal to the person in the passive role. The more a person in the passive role desires a proposal, the more privilege that desire provides for the person in the active role, and vice-versa.

Women start this comparative process at a disadvantage for two reasons. First, fewer women propose than men. Second, fewer men desire proposals than women. Notwithstanding that, the main factor that limits the amount of privilege the active role provides for women is that men place very little, if any, symbolic value on commitment. Commitment has functional value to men, while it has both functional and symbolic value to women.

To use an analogy, the symbolic value of commitment as it relates to the functional value of commitment is similar to how the fragrance of soap relates to its ability to clean. Both men and women value, need, and use soap. The fragrance of soap, however, has far fewer practical applications for men than for women. As a result, consumer product manufacturers make millions selling fragrant soaps and body washes to women while no similar market exists for men. Soap is functional for men and it has very little value beyond its ability to clean. Similarly, both men and women value, need, and use commitment. The symbolic value of commitment in certain social circles, however, has far fewer practical applications for men than for women. Commitment is functional for men: it serves a purpose and has very little symbolic value beyond that purpose. For women, however, commitment has both functional and symbolic value.

For instance, one of the reasons men and women place different values on commitment is because of how each gender gauges the depth and sincerity of the other's intentions. Women place symbolic value on commitment because they gauge the depth and sincerity of a man's interest by his willingness to commit. Men, on the other hand, do not value commitment in this fashion. Men gauge the depth and sincerity of a woman's interest by her willingness to give in to him, which in many cases does not require commitment. And if commitment is required for her to give in to him, it then becomes functional and therefore important to him. This is one of the practical ways in which the difference in the way men and women value commitment impact their decisions about relationships.

Women also place symbolic value on commitment because it exempts them from having to endure oppressive expectations placed on single women by social norms. Socially, a marital commitment is significant because it cloaks a woman with respect by sealing the integrity of her virtue, which allows her to be sexually active without developing a promiscuous reputation. Mind you, there is an entirely different set of oppressive expectations regarding submission that await women once they are married. And as a result, women have begun to change their vows to reflect their interest in marital equality. Notwithstanding that, the fear of being socially stigmatized often prevents single women from being sexually active without a commitment. An informal boyfriend-girlfriend commitment is enough to protect her honor while people assume that she is sexually active.

Commitment also has symbolic importance to women from a religious perspective because it frees them from bearing the burden of sexual purity. Just about every religion in the world calls for sexual purity from its followers. The burden of sexual purity, however, is exacted disproportionately on women because of the social ramifications associated with promiscuity. A marital commitment has symbolic value because it frees women from bearing the burden of sexual purity and the guilt associated with having sex out of wedlock when they depart from bearing that burden.

An informal commitment has enough symbolic value to protect a woman's honor until procreation becomes an issue. When a woman becomes pregnant, however, the only thing that will keep the integrity of her virtue in tact is a formal commitment of exclusivity, which comes in the form of a wedding, a ring, or an engagement to be married. Being pregnant out of wedlock is considered a breach of the integrity of a woman's virtue. The breach is a private matter with public ramifications because the integrity of a woman's virtue is very important to her social standing. Socially, a woman operates under the presumption of virtue until there is public evidence of a breach.

Any woman that receives a proposal after an unexpected pregnancy is going to want to know: "would he want to marry me if I were not pregnant?" This question speaks to a woman's need to be desired, which is a function of her femininity. As a rule of thumb I offer that a woman's femininity will not go without being desired even if her virtue will. A commitment of exclusivity, both formal and informal, has symbolic value because it confirms a woman's desirability while functionally providing companionship.

Also, because of the social and religious interest in keeping a woman's virtue in tact, procreation is tied to marriage. Tying procreation to marriage, however, has a negative impact on a woman's selectivity and standards as she nears the end of her reproductive years. A marital commitment has symbolic value to a woman in the context of procreation because it allows her to achieve motherhood before the end of her reproductive years.

To recap, commitment has symbolic value to women because it offers:

- a means of keeping the integrity of her virtue in tact while sexual activity is assumed,
- freedom from disproportionately bearing the burden of sexual purity,
- freedom from the guilt of having sex out of wedlock,
- confirmation of her desirability through companionship, and
- an opportunity to achieve motherhood before the end of her reproductive years.

Each of these factors increases the value that women have for commitment relative to the value that men have for commitment. The increase in value increases the privilege the active role provides for men relative to the privilege the active role provides for women. Because privilege is the primary determinant of selectivity, and not standards, men have the advantage of being more selective than women when choosing marital partners. The symbolic value women place on commitment provides men with the privilege of unfettered choice when choosing marital partners.

Marital Choice™
$$P_m > P_f$$
P_f equals female privilege
P_m equals male privilege

ANOMALY

A highly privileged female is an anomaly. The privilege in her marital choice will usually exceed the privilege in the marital choice of most men. Visible examples include actresses and/or super models that are extremely attractive and wealthy.

Chapter 6:
The Selectivity Exam
How Selective Are You?

The significant problems we face cannot be solved at the same level of thinking we were at when we created them.

-Albert Einstein

Damon M. Scott

The purpose of the previous chapters was to provide you with a model of how selectivity works. This chapter is designed to provide you with an opportunity to apply the model. The Scott Selectivity Exam™, and its Comparative Analysis component, is a decision analysis model designed to help you evaluate your selectivity by illuminating patterns in your relationship-decisions. The model assumes that you are not married. Please circle your answers to each of the questions provided and tally your scores after completing the exam. After totaling your scores please read carefully through the Comparative Analysis chapter. Good luck with your choices and enjoy your exam.

The Marital Choice

THE SCOTT SELECTIVITY EXAM™

1. Do the majority of the people you date tend to treat you like:
    a. they don't want to disappoint you
    b. let's work it out regardless of who is disappointed
    c. you should not disappoint them
    d. it depends on who I am dealing with
    e. none of the above

2. Do you have standards?
    a. yes
    b. yes, but…
    c. somewhat
    d. I'm not sure
    e. no

3. In general, your attitude about breaking up and moving on can be best described as _____.
    a. reluctant
    b. indifferent
    c. eager
    d. flexible
    e. none of the above

4. Does the person in your life at this moment _____ ?
    a. far exceed your standards
    b. slightly exceed your standards
    c. meet your standards
    d. fall slightly short of meeting your standards
    e. fall far short of meeting your standards

5. How privileged are you?
    a. highly
    b. above average
    c. average
    d. low
    e. none/non-existent

6. Would you rather be with someone that _____ ?
   a. loves you more than you love them
   b. you love more than they love you
   c. loves you just as much as you love them

7. When a struggle arises for control of the relationship, do you usually _____ ?
   a. struggle to maintain control
   b. struggle to win control
   c. flex to exert control
   d. relinquish control
   e. none of the above

8. Of the people you have dated in the past, how many of them met your standards?
   a. all of them
   b. most of them
   c. some of them
   d. one of them
   e. none of them

9. During the times when someone rejected you did you _____ ?
   a. wonder why they were not interested
   b. wonder why you did not measure up
   c. assume you know why
   d. not wonder at all
   e. none of the above

10. Have you ever been intimate with someone that fell short of meeting your standards?
    a. no, my standards would not allow
    b. no, my needs have never been such that I've had to
    c. yes, I could have done better though
    d. yes, my needs took precedence over my standards
    e. yes, my options left me with no other alternative

The Marital Choice

11. Does your privilege tend to provide you with _____ ?
    a. so many options that you become indifferent to them
    b. enough options that you can pick and choose
    c. enough options to enjoy yourself when you need to
    d. not really enough to do what you want to do
    e. none of the above

12. Would you say that most of the people you have rejected in the past _____ ?
    a. exceeded your standards
    b. met your standards
    c. did not meet your standards
    d. not applicable/you haven't really rejected anyone

13. Which of the following comes the closest to describing the reasons for why people have fallen in love with you?
    a. because of how you treated them
    b. because they were smitten with you regardless of how you treated them
    c. because of the chemistry you had together
    d. it depends on who I was with

14. Would you benefit from being _____ ?
    a. more self-centered
    b. less self-centered

15. How demanding are you?
    a. considerably   (all the time)
    b. moderately   (most of the time)
    c. fairly   (I've got my moments)
    d. adequately   (I can be when I need to be)
    e. not at all

16. When you learn that someone doesn't meet your standards, do you usually _____ ?
    a. end the relationship and move on
    b. keep that person around though you've lost interest
    c. discuss it with them and how it affects your interest in them
    d. try to change them to meet your standards
    e. none of the above

17. Do you feel you have any control over the quality of people you meet and consider to date?
    a. no, I am lucky if I meet a good person
    b. no, I know what I want I just can't seem to find it
    c. yes, I know how to attract the type of person I want
    d. yes, I attract enough people that I can pick and choose who I deal with

18. Would you say that the majority of the people you have been with in the past were people that _____ ?
    a. pursued you
    b. you pursued

19. How many people have you been intimate with that fell short of meeting your standards?
    a. none of them
    b. one of them
    c. some of them
    d. most of them
    e. all of them

20. Most of my relationships have been with people that _____ ?
    a. loved me more than I loved them
    b. I loved more than they loved me
    c. loved me just as much as I loved them

21. Is the person in your life now _____ ?
    a. more privileged than you
    b. less privileged than you
    c. just as privileged as you

22. Do you feel, or have you ever felt, exempt from having to work for the affections of others?
    a. all of the time
    b. most of the time
    c. frequently
    d. some of the time
    e. none of the time

The Marital Choice

23. Rejecting people tends to make me feel _____.
    a. uncomfortable
    b. guilty
    c. neither
    d. good

24. Of the people you have dated, how many of them were totally enamored or smitten with you?
    a. none of them
    b. one of them
    c. some of them
    d. most of them
    e. all of them

25. Do the people you date generally _____ ?
    a. know what you like and know that they are it
    b. know what you like and know that they are not it
    c. not know what you like, though they are it
    d. not know what you like because they are not it

26. When someone rejects you do you tend to _____?
    a. think, "their loss"
    b. persist
    c. accept it
    d. become indifferent
    e. none of the above

27. Who I date usually depends on _____.
    a. my standards
    b. my needs
    c. more a than b
    d. more b than a
    e. neither

28. Does your level of privilege tend to make exclusivity _____ ?
    a. impractical or unrealistic
    b. difficult or troublesome
    c. competitive but doable
    d. practical and realistic
    e. preferred and sought after

29. To what extent do you utilize your standards?
    a. 100% - I have them and I use them, no exceptions.
    b. 80% - I have them but I stray below them sometimes
    c. 60% - I have them but I stray below them most times
    d. 40% - I have them but I use them sporadically
    e. 20% - I have them but I don't use them

30. How often do people make advances at you?
    a. never
    b. some of the time
    c. frequently
    d. most of the time
    e. all of the time

31. How high are your standards?
    a. high
    b. above average
    c. average
    d. low
    e. none/non-existent

32. How resilient are you after a break-up?
    a. considerably
    b. moderately
    c. fairly
    d. adequately
    e. not very

33. Looking back at your choices, can you say that your standards have _____ ?
    a. trended upward
    b. trended downward
    c. fallen off the face of the earth
    d. suddenly come alive
    e. been all over the place

34. Which would be easier for you?
    a. to tell someone they do not meet your standards
    b. to get someone that does meet your standards

35. How durable are your standards?
    a. like a brick wall
    b. like an iron rod
    c. like a diving board
    d. like a line in the sand
    e. like water

36. Do you meet the standards you have for others?
    a. yes
    b. yes, but…
    c. somewhat
    d. I'm not sure
    e. no/not applicable

37. How confident are you?
    a. very
    b. above average
    c. average
    d. below average
    e. not very

38. How many relationships have you started or re-started immediately after a bad break-up?
    a. all of them
    b. most of them
    c. some of them
    d. one of them
    e. none of them

39. Do you meet the standards you have set for yourself?
    a. yes
    b. yes, but…
    c. somewhat
    d. I'm not sure
    e. no/not applicable

40. How often are you intimate with someone that does not meet your standards?
    a. all of the time
    b. most of the time
    c. some of the time
    d. rarely
    e. none of the time

41. How have you been treated in your past relationships? For the most part, can you say that you have been _____?
    a. tolerated
    b. celebrated
    c. accepted
    d. badgered
    e. hustled

42. Of the people you have shared relationships with, were most of them people that you _____?
    a. tolerated
    b. celebrated
    c. accepted
    d. badgered
    e. hustled

43. How many times have you made a permanent decision based on a temporary situation in your relationships?
    a. never
    b. once
    c. more than once
    d. a few times
    e. several times

44. If you married the person in your life at this moment would you be _____?
    a. marrying up
    b. marrying down
    c. settling
    d. marrying your equal or your partner
    e. marrying your princess or prince charming

The Marital Choice

45. Would you be comfortable making a marital choice given the way that you make relationship-decisions?
    a. yes
    b. no

THE END
PLEASE CALCULATE YOUR SCORES
AND PROCEED TO THE NEXT CHAPTER ON
COMPARATIVE ANALYSIS

Question Number	a.	b.	c.	d.	e.	Your Score
1	4	3	1	2	-	
3	3	1	2	4	-	
5	84-76	75-59	58-42	41-25	24-8	No score. Compare your prediction to final score
7	3	2	4	1	-	
9	3	2	1	4	-	
11	4	3	2	1	-	
13	2	4	3	1	-	
15	4	3	2	1	-	
17	1	2	3	4	-	
18 (Female)	3	4	-	-	-	
18 (Male)	4	3	-	-	-	
20	3	2	4	-	-	
22	4	3	2	1	-	
24	-	1	2	3	4	
26	2	3	4	1	-	
28	4	3	2	1	-	
30	-	1	2	3	4	
32	4	3	2	1	-	
34	3	4	-	-	-	
37	4	3	2	1	-	
39	4	3	2	1	-	
41	2	4	3	1	-	
44	1	2	-	3	4	
45	no score	no score	no score	no score	no score	
Total						

The Marital Choice

Question Number	a.	b.	c.	d.	e.	Your Score
2	4	3	2	1	-	
4	2	3	4	1	-	
6	3	2	4	-	-	
8	4	3	2	1	-	
10	4	3	2	1	-	
12	3	4	2	-	-	
14	2	4	-	-	-	
16	3	2	4	1	-	
19	4	3	2	1	-	
21	2	3	4	-	-	
23	2	1	4	3	-	
25	4	2	3	1	-	
27	4	1	3	2	-	
29	4	3	2	1	-	
31	84-76	75-59	58-42	41-25	24-8	No score. Compare your prediction to final score
33	4	2	-	3	1	
35	4	3	2	1	-	
36	4	3	2	1	-	
38	-	1	2	3	4	
40	-	1	2	3	4	
42	2	4	3	1	-	
43	4	3	2	1	-	
Total						

Privilege Score	Ranges	Your Score
High	84 76	
Above Average	75 59	
Average	58 42	
Below Average	41 25	
Low	24 8	

Standard Score	Ranges	Your Score
High	84 76	
Above Average	75 59	
Average	58 42	
Below Average	41 25	
Low	24 8	

Your Level of Selectivity		
Highly	84 76	
Above Average	75 59	
Average	58 42	
Below Average	41 25	
Low	24 8	

Chapter 7:
The Comparative Analysis Model
The Patterns in Your Relationship Decisions

There is a wealth of information hidden in your exam responses and comparative analysis is designed to provide you with access to that information. The analysis will focus on your standards, privilege, and your selectivity. Let's start with your standards.

STANDARDS ANALYSIS SECTION

How does your standard score compare to the score range provided by your answer to question 31? If your standard score is within the score range provided by question 31 then this suggests that your beliefs about your standards are accurate. As a result, you can skip to the analysis section on privilege. If your standard score exceeds or falls short of the score range provided by question 31 then you have a fail-rate, which suggests that your beliefs about your standards may not be accurate.

THE FAIL-RATE

Mathematically, your fail-rate is the difference between your standard score and the highest or lowest number in the score range provided by question 31. If your standard score exceeds the score range provided by question 31 then subtract your standard score from the highest number in the score range to get a positive fail-rate. If your standard score is less than the score range then subtract the lowest number in the range from your standard score to get a negative fail-rate.

THE POSITIVE FAIL-RATE

If your standard score exceeds the score range provided by question 31 your fail-rate is positive. A positive fail-rate means that your standards are actually higher than you predicted in question 31. The question is why? What would make you believe that your standards are lower than they actually are? A positive fail-rate is not unfortunate. It is best, however, that your beliefs about your standards are accurate.

THE NEGATIVE FAIL-RATE

If your standard score falls short of the score range provided by question 31 you have a negative fail-rate. A negative fail-rate can be explained in one of two ways. Either you have overestimated your standards or you have standards but you are not utilizing them. If the latter is the case, the question is why? Do you lack the privilege to exercise your standards? Or, do you lack the nerve to pursue or require what you want? Regardless of the reason, by consistently deciding not to exercise your standards you have developed a decision-pattern of pursuing or accepting less than you want.

THE NEGATIVE FAIL-RATE PERCENTAGE

Converting the negative fail-rate into a positive number and dividing by your standard score will produce a fail-rate percentage, which predicts the extent to which your standards are unfulfilled. So, for example, let's assume that your standard score is {54} and the score range provided by question number 31 is {84-76}. Your fail-rate is -22 {54-76} and your fail-rate percentage is 41% {22/54}, which indicates that a material part of your relationship-decisions, almost half, are below your standards based on your responses. If, however, your standard score is 68 and the score range provided by question 31 is {84-76}, your fail-rate is {-8} and your fail-rate percentage is {12%}. As such, this fail-rate indicates that approximately a tenth of your relationship-decisions are below your standards based on your exam responses. Please calculate the following.

Standard Score	
Question 31 Score Range	
Fail Rate	
Fail Rate Percentage	

PRIVILEGE ANALYSIS SECTION

If your privilege score is within the range provided by question 5 then this suggests that your beliefs about your level of privilege is accurate. As a result, you can skip to the next analysis section. If your privilege score is outside of the score range provided by question 5 you have a fail-rate, which suggests that your beliefs about your level of privilege may not be accurate.

THE POSITIVE FAIL-RATE

A positive fail-rate means that you have a higher level of privilege than you predicted in your response to question 5. The question is why? What would make you believe that your level of privilege is lower than its current level? While a positive fail-rate is not unfortunate, it can affect how you exercise your standards.

THE NEGATIVE FAIL-RATE

You have a negative fail-rate if your privilege score falls short of the score range provided by question 5. A negative fail-rate for your privilege score can be explained in one of two ways. Either you have overestimated your privilege, or your privilege is underutilized. If the latter is accurate you have developed a decision-pattern of not asserting yourself at the maximum level of your privilege. This is excellent if your standards are being met at this level of privilege. If not, however, why not exercise greater privilege by raising your standards? Is there something that makes you feel guilty about your level of privilege? Do you lack the nerve to exercise higher standards or the interest in dealing with all that comes along with that? Underutilized privilege usually indicates that you have voluntarily set your standards artificially low.

In the case of either fail-rate focus your analysis on your responses to the standard or privilege questions to see the consistencies, contradictions, and patterns in your decisions. Please calculate the following.

Privilege Score	
Question 5 Score Range	
Fail Rate	
Fail Rate Percentage	

If you have negative fail-rates for your privilege and standard scores then it is possible that, by definition, you are settling.

SELECTIVITY ANALYSIS SECTION

Compare your privilege score to your standard score. If the range of your privilege score equals or exceeds the range of your standard score ($P \geq S =$ **Selective**™) your relationship-decision are selective and your selectivity equals the range of your standard score. If your privilege exceeds your standards and the two are in different score ranges your standards may be too low.

If the range of your standard score exceeds the range of your privilege score **(S > P = Not Selective™)** your relationship-decision are not selective and your selectivity equals the range of your privilege score, indicating that your standards are overreaching your privilege. If your standard score exceeds your privilege score but is still within the same score range the difference is negligible. Your selectivity range should be compared to your response to question number 3 in the Selectivity Exam™ Pre-Test, which represents your early prediction about your level of selectivity. The score ranges for the pre-test responses are the same as those for questions 5 and 31. Please compare the following.

Standard Score	
Privilege Score	
Selectivity Range Score	
Selectivity Range Score Predicted in Pre-Test Question 3	

THE COMPARATIVE ANALYSIS CONCLUDING QUESTIONS

Just when you thought the exam was over, the real work starts. Only you can do the comparative analysis for your unique set of exam responses. While you may be wondering how to start, there is actually a methodical process you can follow. Start with your response to question number 2 and begin comparing all the responses in numerical order to that response. When you find a comparison that seems like a contradiction or a paradox, use it to form a question, which you then try to explain or resolve.

For example, one analysis led to conflicts between responses {4d, 27a, and 29a}. These responses created the question, "if the person you date usually depends on your standards and you utilize your standards all of the time {27a-29a}, how is it that the person in your life now falls short of meeting your standards {4d}?" Continuing the analysis yielded the set {6a,15a-21b}, which revealed that the person had a pattern of being very demanding {15a} with others that were not as privileged {21b} but who loved them more {6a}. This is exactly the type of decision-pattern the exam was designed to reveal.

The key is to question your decisions relentlessly to identify unproductive decision-patterns and make them productive. Do not question circumstances, people, or motives, or you will loose focus of the purpose of comparative analysis, which is to bring the full weight of your judgment down on your decisions. Put all of your conclusions in the form of the comparative analysis concluding questions. 1) *Have I decided* to... 2) *Is this decision* acceptable? *What decision* would be acceptable? 3) How can I position myself to *make that decision?*"

For instance, let's assume you had the answer set {4d-6a-11a-15a-21b}, with which you were not happy. Do not ask yourself, "am I in a relationship of convenience?" Every question should have some version of the word decision in it to keep your focus on your decisions. The comparative analysis questions would be, "*have I decided* to be in a relationship of convenience?" "*Is this decision* acceptable to me? *What decision* would be acceptable to me? How can I position myself to *make that decision?*" These questions keep the focus on your decisions and the analysis directed towards making the next best decision. Good luck with your analysis.

**Chapter 8:
Privilege & The Power of the Passive Role**

Up to this point we have focused primarily on the impact that privilege has on the active role. This chapter focuses on the power that privilege brings to the passive role. In defining selectivity the first chapter indicated that privilege was needed to exercise choice at a level commensurate with your standards. All things considered equal, the higher your standards the more privilege needed to exercise choice.

Privilege has the same fundamental impact on the passive role as it does on the active role: it makes the difference between having standards and exercising a choice with those standards. In either role, having standards simply means that you have decided what you want. Here is the difference, however. Exercising a choice in the active role means that you have the ability to get what you want. Exercising a choice in the passive role, however, means that you have the ability to *attract* what you want.

In the passive role you don't choose, you are the one being chosen. So, if someone chooses you by approaching you, making a pass at you, or extending an invitation for a date it is because they are attracted to you for some reason. That reason is the source of your privilege. In this manner, privilege provides choice in the passive role just as it does in the active role.

The primary benefit of being in the active role is being able to exercise selectivity, which means being able to choose the person you want from all of your available options. The selection-decision is only half of the process, however. After the selection-decision is made the person in the passive role has the privilege of accepting, declining, or staying the selection-decision, and therein lies its power.

The Marital Choice

The primary benefit of being in the passive role is being able to exercise standards, which means having the power to attract and reject anyone that does not measure up to your standards. All things considered equal, the higher your privilege the higher your standards can be.

Standards precede privilege in the active role because you start out with what you want and then you exercise your privilege by choosing. As such, for the active role we say the higher your standards the more privilege needed to exercise your selection-choice. The same is true for the passive role just in reverse order. Privilege precedes standards in the passive role because you start out with others being attracted to you and choosing you because of your privilege. After being chosen you then exercise your standards through your standard-choice. As such, for the passive role we say the higher your privilege the higher your standards can be.

The clearest example of this can be seen in situations where a woman has received several proposals but has not accepted any. In this case, her privilege has allowed her to set her standards so high that no one has been able to meet them. Let's consider a practical example of how exercising standards work in the passive role and equate that example to a marital choice.

Consider Yale Law School. Once the admissions process starts and applications are placed before the admissions board they have some important standard-decisions to make. They must accept, decline, or stay some students. Because of the limited space in the class, the rigors of the curriculum, and the impact admissions standards have on the school's reputation the admissions officers have to accept the most competitive candidates in the applicant pool. The standards are exceptionally high for the standard-decisions the admissions officers must make. Let's consider Yale's privilege.

Yale is generally considered one of the most prestigious law schools in the world with former Presidents, as well as other world leaders, credited to its list of alumni. As a result, the school has the privilege to exercise exceptionally high standards. Among its privileges are its reputation, prestige, and the power of its alumni network. As a result, the school is able to attract thousands of highly qualified candidates from all over the world. And because it can attract exceptional candidates it is able to exercise its highest standards.

Let's assume that Yale did not have its privilege. Would it still be able to exercise exceptionally high standards? No, because without its privilege it would not be able to attract a pool of candidates that met its standards. Without its privilege it would have to exercise standard-choices with lower standards. Or worse, it could have exceptionally high standards while attracting marginally competitive students and no one would be qualified to sit in the class. The school is able to exercise high standards because it has high privileges.

Decisions that exercise high standards in the passive role are those where your privilege meets or exceeds your standards, no matter how high your standards. Decisions where privilege meets or exceeds standards are expressed as:

$$P \geq S = \text{High Standards}^{\text{TM}}$$

The Marital Choice

Equating this decision to a marital choice, if you are in the passive role and your privilege is greater than or equal to your standards, you have the ability to attract people that meet or exceed your standards. And because you have the privilege to attract those that meet or exceed your standards, you have the power to exercise your highest standards.

Decisions that exercise low standards are those where your standards exceed your privilege. Decisions where your standards exceed your privilege is expressed as:

$$S > P = \text{Low Standards}^{TM}$$

Equating this decision to a marital choice, if you are in the passive role and your standards exceed your privilege you do not have the ability to attract those that meet your standards. And because you cannot attract those that meet your standards you can only exercise your standards on those that do not meet your standards. As a result, you cannot exercise your highest standards.

The tragedy of not being privileged in the passive role is in only knowing the power of genuine rejection and never knowing the power of genuine acceptance. Genuine rejection is defined here as the experience of rejecting someone that does not meet your standards, while genuine acceptance is the experience of accepting someone that meets or exceeds your standards. As such, rejecting someone that meets or exceeds your standards is not genuine rejection. By the same token, accepting someone that does not meet your standards is not genuine acceptance.

Exercising genuine acceptance is an experience unique to those who are privileged enough to attract those that meet or exceed their standards. Not knowing the power of genuine acceptance is a tough reality because it means never getting all of what you want, which is one of the most aggravating aspects of the selection process.

Participation in the Passive Role

There are two ways to participate in the passive role of the marital-selection-process: actively or passively. People who participate actively use their influence over the person in the active role to materially affect the outcome and timeline of the process. For example, in one case the passive participant was a woman. Not long after meeting her boyfriend she determined that she wanted to marry him. Interesting enough, she was a consultant that claimed to have a strategy for everything. Her stated strategy for her boyfriend was to show him how great it was to be with her and then to threaten to take it all away, making sure that he was aware of other men who were interested in being with her in the event of their brake-up. She executed her plan and he proposed. In this situation she was an active participant in the passive role of the marital-selection-process.

Many women remark, "it's always the manipulative women who get the guy rather than the nice ones." This has its merit. In focusing on bad intentions, however, the critique overlooks the effectiveness of actively engaging in the process. That a woman could "manipulate" a man into proposing means that she is aware of her influence and that she is willing to use it to achieve her goal. The same is true of men in the passive role. It is not that "nice guys finish last", it is just that men who actively engage in the process use their influence effectively. Interesting enough, most guys that are considered "dogs" actually participate in the selection process from the passive role because they are privileged enough to have many women pursue them.

Notwithstanding that, people that participate passively in the passive role respond only to the efforts of the person in the active role by affirming or denying their advances as the relationship progresses. The hallmark of the passive participant is that they have no material affect on timeline or the outcome of the marital-selection-process. The unobtrusive participation is by design because among the lion's share of passive participants are traditionalists who feel it is their rite-of-passage to be wooed into receiving a marriage proposal. To participate actively in the process would be beneath them. One woman who was a devout Christian described that the extent of her participation was affirming or denying the efforts of her mate. Even though she really wanted to marry him, she could not bring herself to do anything more. There are several reasons for why people participate passively in the passive role of the process. Under such circumstances, however, the success of the selection process relies largely on the efforts of the participant in the active role.

**Chapter 9:
The Impact of Love on Selectivity**

Love is not finding the perfect person, but finding the imperfect person perfect.
　　　　　　　　　　　　　　　　　　　　　　　　**-unknown*

One of the most fascinating aspects of being in love is that it frees you from want. People spend so much of their lives wanting through their standards that they never take into consideration the impact that being free of want can have on their lives. The emotional rush of being in love does not come from the satisfaction of having all of your standards met. Rather, the rush comes from the lifting of your spirits as love frees you from the encumbrance of your wants, standards, and all of the experiences that developed them. Therein lies the healing and euphoria of love. The resulting emotions are just intense devotion and adoration, not for someone who met all of your standards, but for someone who freed you from wanting anything. As such, we say that love is blind and true love asks for nothing. Also, there is no failing in love because in order to fail you must first have to want.

Love factors standards out of the selection process leaving only privilege, which is in essence who you are, a bundle of characteristics. Selectivity cancels with standards because the lack of want eliminates the desire and need to select.

$$\frac{(\cancel{Standards} + Privilege = \cancel{Selectivity}^{TM})}{\cancel{Standards}}$$

$$= Privilege$$

The implication of which is that if you find yourself in want not only are you not in love but you are still engaged in the selection process, even if you have committed to an exclusive relationship.

Chapter 10:
The Origin of the Marital-Selection-Process

...all the foundations of the earth are out of course...

-Psalms 82:5

The first wedding in human history commenced with a rather unorthodoxed selection process. Genesis 2:18, 21-25 states:

> "*¹⁸The LORD God said that it is not good that man should be alone. I will make a mate suitable for him. ²¹So the LORD God caused a deep sleep to fall upon the man, and while he slept he took one of his ribs and closed up its place with flesh. ²²And the rib which the LORD God had taken from the man he made into a woman and brought her to the man. ²³Then the man said this is at last bone of my bones and flesh of my flesh; she shall be called Woman because she was taken out of man. ²⁴Therefore a man leaves his father and his mother and cleaves to his wife, and they become one flesh. ²⁵And the man and his wife were both naked and were not ashamed." KJV*

In Genesis 2:22 Eve was created and presented to Adam. The rules of marriage were explained in Genesis 2:24 and Adam and Eve were pronounced man and wife in Genesis 2:25 concluding the first marriage in human history. While Eve was a passive participant in the creative process, she was in neither the active or passive role. God was in the active role in that he selected Eve by creating her for Adam, who was in the passive role. Eve was presented to Adam, which provided him with an opportunity to exercise his standards. Adam exercised his standards by saying, "…at last…". By that response you would have thought Eve was the most beautiful woman in the world, and at the time she was.

By comparing verses in Genesis and Proverbs we are able to see the effects of sin on relationships. In Genesis 2:22 the woman is created and brought to the man. In Genesis 24:7-67 the woman is selected and brought to the man. The certainty with which people connected in Genesis, however, seems to have faded in Proverbs 18:22 because it reads, "whoso finds a wife finds a good thing and

The Marital Choice

obtains the favor of the Lord". What accounts for the change in the level of certainty?

The marital-selection-process was created with the fall of man from the Garden of Eden. The fall of man created the one characteristic that is essential for the marital-selection-process to exist: uncertainty, ...as to whether people would connect and uncertainty of the quality of people available to connect. The practical problem with sin is that it creates an opportunity and a means for human behavior to vary with the will and word of God. Variability in human behavior from God's will, or sin, introduced risk to all forms of human relationships and created a world where trust was necessary to facilitate human interaction.

Without uncertainty, there is no need to trust. Without uncertainty, there is no need to have faith or confidence, hope, ...or belief. Without uncertainty there is no difference between what should be and what is, and as a result there would also be no need for integrity and honesty.

Without uncertainty in human behavior there is no need for contracts, attorneys, or the rule of law. Without uncertainty there is no risk, and as such, no need for insurance, credit, fund managers, underwriters, commercial and investment bankers, or capital and stock markets. Without uncertainty there is no need for audited financial statements and certified public accountants. Without uncertainty there is no such thing as fear, lying, infidelity, unfaithfulness, broken hearts, or emotional pain because without uncertainty there is no such thing as an expectation, there is just interaction. Without uncertainty there is no such thing as being insecure. Waiting to exhale becomes unnecessary if there is no uncertainty. Uncertainty created every challenge we face in human relationships, romantic or otherwise, from the Garden of Eden to Wall Street.

In romance, people try to eliminate the uncertainty of connecting, or the risk of being alone, by dating more than one person. This is a rational, common sense choice that people make to manage risks that affect their emotions. The uncertainty of people connecting can be significantly reduced with volume and diversity because connecting is a numbers game for the most part. If you date enough people eventually you will find someone with whom you connect.

The uncertainty of the quality of people available to connect, however, can never be eliminated because people will never be perfect. This uncertainty creates the risk of emotional loss and the need for people to trust, which can be incredibly difficult for some to do, particularly if they have already been hurt. As a result, some try to eliminate the need to trust by dating more than one person to avoid emotional attachment. But because people are not perfect, trust will always be an essential part of human interaction.

A material part of dating is figuring out who you can trust, which, again, is just a form of risk management. The people you date represent a portfolio of relationships in which you have varying degrees of emotional interest. Some people only become involved with those that are safe alternatives for them. Some people marry in this fashion. Others that can afford an emotional loss assume the risk of becoming involved with the person they really want. Each choice is an instinctive attempt to manage the risk of emotional loss, or the fear of being hurt, which would not be necessary without the existence of uncertainty.

Man's exile from the Garden of Eden also created the problem of scarcity, an external effect of sin on relationships that is found in Genesis 3:17-19. Scarcity created external privilege such as wealth, affluence, and power. Without scarcity and the uncertainty of well being it produces, there would be no such thing as rich or poor, which would eliminate the phrase, "for richer or for poorer". Privilege equals eligibility {**P=E**}™ in a world of scarce resources because it reduces the uncertainty of well being that people work so hard to eliminate in their lives, and with their marital choices. Many people want to achieve financial security. First, notice that "security" is a word that pertains to risk and uncertainty. Second, the goal itself is just an objective to eliminate the uncertainty of well being, which is an effect of sin.

Again, the problem with introducing sin to humanity is that it creates uncertainty in human interaction, which produces risk. There is no evidence anywhere to suggest that uncertainty was ever intended to be a part of our lives, let alone a material part of our romantic lives. Faith in God was designed to eliminate the effects of uncertainty and risk in human interaction.

Before the fall of man there was no risk of uncertainty because there was no sin to allow human behavior to vary with the will and word of God. Several chapters after the fall of man in the 24th chapter of Genesis Abraham relies on his covenant with God to eliminate the risk of uncertainty when selecting a wife for Isaac.

Proverbs 18:22, however, acknowledges the risk of uncertainty by stating, "whoso finds a wife finds a good thing and obtains the favor of the Lord ". By offering the favor of the Lord as an incentive for marriage, Proverbs 18:22 suggests that God's involvement comes at the end of the marital-selection-process and not at the beginning as illustrated in Genesis 24.

Proverbs 18:22 also suggests that each gender has a specific role in the marital-selection-process. By stating that the woman should be "found" Proverbs 18:22 implies that the passive role was created for the woman. The inference is that women were only meant to be chosen, and therefore never meant to be more selective than men when choosing marital partners.

We close with a hypothesis about the ideal order of the marital-selection-process. One of the most fascinating aspects of conducting Biblical research, particularly if you read through large sections of the Bible in relatively short periods of time, is that you begin to notice patterns in God's selection-decisions (see Gideon, Joseph, Moses, David, et cetera). Though God works in mysterious ways and his thoughts are far above ours, even his decisions have some discernible patterns, which undoubtedly is by design. There is an order that has been repeated at least once. And though twice does make a pattern, the process seems to be unique enough to happen only by deliberate design.

Whenever God gets involved in the marital-selection-process a specific order seems to take place. God is in the active role, man is in the passive role, and the woman is a passive participant in the process though she is in neither role. The order has appeared in the formation of two couples: Adam & Eve and Isaac & Rebekah in the 24th chapter of Genesis. These couples are significant because one was formed before the fall of man when everything was perfect and the other was formed after with the presence of sin and uncertainty in human interaction. Yet, God's involvement seemed to produce the same pattern of order, which suggests that God is constant despite the impact of our choices on our fate.

Abraham initiated the process for Isaac & Rebekah by saying to his servant, "do not select a woman from Canaan, but go into my country and select a wife for my son" (Genesis 24:3). At this point the marital-selection-process was in place because there were several women to choose from, uncertainty as to which would be selected, and uncertainty about the quality of those available to connect. In Genesis 24:7 Abraham makes it clear that the Lord would send his Angels to show his servant the exact woman to select as Isaac's wife. As with Adam & Eve, God got involved and selected Rebekah, who was then brought to Isaac.

The most significant question that can come from a pattern of God's involvement in the marital-selection-process is the question of who has the primary responsibility of choosing: man, woman, or God? The pattern of God's involvement in the process seems to indicate a preference for the active role, which in layman's terms means that if God is involved then God is in charge.

An earlier chapter indicated that men were more selective than women when choosing marital partners because norms suggests that the marital-selection-process was not designed for women to make selection-decisions. The pattern of God's involvement, however, seems to suggest that the marital-selection-process was not designed for men to make selection-decisions either. Sociological norms seem to place men and women in the active and passive roles, respectively. The order of the marital-selection-process with God's involvement, however, seems to put God in the active role, man in the passive role, and the woman as a passive participant in the entire process.

Finally, the most pertinent question is how do we get God to eliminate the uncertainty in our marital-selection-process? The answer is simple. Believe. Again, faith in God was designed to eliminate the effects of uncertainty in our lives. Abraham demonstrates this clearly by relying on his covenant with God to eliminate the uncertainty in his son's marital-selection-process[1]. Also, the issue of whether there would ever be any uncertainty in God was important enough that he addressed directly when he said to Malachi, "I am the Lord. *I change not*[2]". With that unchanging nature God speaks in absolutes by saying that, "*all* things are possible to him that believes[3]; *every* place your foot shall tread I have given you; *no* man shall be able to stand in your way[4]; *no* weapon formed against you shall prosper; *every* tongue that rises against you in judgment thou shalt condemn; *this is the heritage of the servants of the Lord, and their righteousness is of me*, saith the Lord[5]". Having faith in God will eliminate the uncertainty in your marital-selection-process and, more importantly, in your life.

---

[1] Genesis 24, the entire chapter
[2] Malachi 3:6
[3] Mark 9:23
[4] Joshua 1:3,5
[5] Isaiah 54:17. Italicized to indicate the requirement of right standing with God to eliminate uncertainty. See Matthew 6:33 and Hebrews 11:6.

**Chapter 11:
Epilogue**

What lies behind and before us are tiny matters compared to what lies within us.

-Ralph Waldo Emerson

By now you should have gotten a good look at:

1. how selectivity works;
2. the factors that impact selectivity;
3. the patterns in your relationship-decisions;
4. your standards and privilege;
5. your level of selectivity;
6. the impact of love on selectivity;
7. the impact of God's involvement in the marital-selection-process;

The effect of getting a good look at these factors should have been similar to the effect of seeing a budget that traces your spending. You learn valuable information about how you are allocating your resources. Are you surprised at what you have found? Or, have you confirmed what you already know? The resources referred to here are invaluable: time, love, care, effort, dignity, virtue, self-respect, self-esteem, and ultimately faith and confidence in yourself. Time is of particular importance because once you spend it you cannot get it back. Are you squandering your resources? Are your relationship-decisions getting you what you want? If you are interested in marriage, can you rely on your current pattern of relationship-decisions to make an impeccable marital choice? If so, good, you are ahead of the game. If not, change your decisions. It's just like the joke where the patient says, "doctor, it hurts when I do that". And the doctor replies, "then don't do that".

The quality of your experiences in your relationships is a result of the quality of your standard and selection-choices. And while the tendency is to believe that these choices are made only at the beginning of the relationship, the truth is that they are made at the end of each stage of the relationship and mark the beginning of a new stage where you have either grown closer or further apart. You start by selecting or accepting someone to date and it escalates to selecting or accepting that person for friendship, and again for intimacy, and again for exclusivity, and again for marriage, though not necessarily in that order with those outcomes.

A proposal is a selection-choice verbalized at the end of your informal dating relationship. The standard-choice marks the beginning of a new stage in the relationship where you have either grown closer or further apart. During the course of a relationship "putting up with something" is just a matter of accepting treatment that is below your standards. Accepting sub-par treatment is a standard-choice that marks the beginning of a new stage where you have either grown closer or further apart. When the same decision is made in a pattern, as they often are, most people grow apart without realizing that they have decided to grow apart. Standard and selection-decisions are made constantly throughout a relationship and when you control the quality of those decisions your expectations become much more realistic about your relationship, which drastically increases the quality of your experience.

Finally, a tenth chapter that pays homage to the awesome and benevolent power of God anchors The Marital Choice™. The intent was the leave you in the same place the author had to go for insight, self-analysis, and decision-analysis. To change a decision you need only the power to change your mind. To change a pattern of decisions, however, you need the power of God. God bless you in your relationship-decisions and in, particularly, your marital choice.

Relationship-Selection-Process Glossary

Active role: the segment of the relationship-selection-process from which the selection-choice is made and selectivity is exercised.

Caliber of standards: a specific level of adequacy, sufficiency, or acceptability.

Durability of standards: the extent to which a specific level of adequacy, sufficiency, or acceptability is resistant to compromise, concession, or negotiation.

External Privilege: extrinsic characteristics or factors that increase the ability to exercise choice commensurate with standards.

Genuine acceptance: allowing someone in your life that meets or exceeds your standards. *Antonym: disingenuous acceptance*

Genuine rejection: not allowing someone in your life that does not meet your standards.

Internal Privilege: intrinsic characteristics that increase the ability to exercise choice commensurate with standards.

Martial Choice: a distinct or discrete judgment to select or accept a spouse.

Negative fail-rate: an indication of overestimated or underutilized standards or privilege.

Passive role: the segment of the relationship-selection-process from which the standard-choice is made and standards are exercised.

Positive fail-rate: an underestimation of standards or privilege.

Privilege of Unfettered Choice: the advantage of final authority.

Selective: the state or quality of a choice that exercises privilege commensurate with standards.

Selection-decision: a distinct or discrete judgment indicating preference or interest in initiating a relationship.

Standard-decision: a distinct or discrete judgment to accept, decline, or stay a selection-decision.

The mark of a true intellectual, a true contributor, is not whether you are right or wrong, or whether your point succeeds, but whether you generate a debate.

Ashley Montague